LIZZIE

AND THE BIRDS

To Ben and Danny -
Onwards and upwards!

Lizzie and the Birds
Published by Prim-Ed Publishing 2018
Copyright© Dawn and Mick Robertson 2018

Prim-Ed Publishing
Marshmeadows
New Ross
County Wexford
Y34 TA46

PR-6227
ISBN: 978-1-84654-921-2

Copyright Information

www.prim-ed.com

 Lucky Duckie

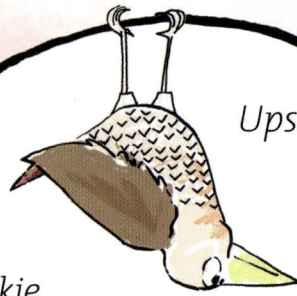 Upside-down Bird

Rollerbird

Bluebeak

 Minerbird

 Snowy

Worm mine

 Eco

Cheeky

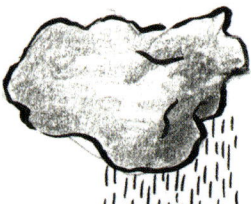

Crow

Mystery Bird

Rainbow Bird

Marvin Muscles

2

Postit

Ghostie

Rob the Builder

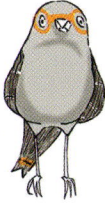
Clementeeny

Bananas

We are the Dawn Chorus

Superbird

Knight

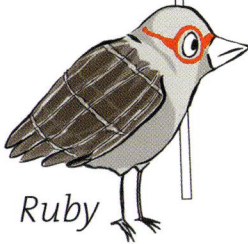
TWIGS

Ruby

Plum

Chiff and Chaff
(the yes-no birds)

DAWN CHORUS RULE OK

Boy Blue

Wizzling

Egglet

3

Lizzie and Dad loved their new house,
overlooking snowy mountains,
close to a bubbling stream
and an enchanted swimming spot.

Everything was perfect,
except for one thing …

... Lizzie was desperate to find some new friends because she felt so lonely. She imagined what they'd be like.

Dan is the cheekiest boy in the world! He makes me laugh.

Ruby is the best friend EVER! She is kind and patient.

Here I am with my amazing friends.

Prince Marvin is strong and spotty.

Rakash Beckle would protect our crew from any dangers.

Poppy writes me secret messages and is caring.

Super Ben is an acrobat and he's teaching me to cartwheel.

Wanda is a whizz at magic.

One night, whilst she was dreaming about their fabulous adventures, an angry storm blew in from the snowy mountains and began to wail and gust and roar!

And it's fiercer than a ...

Muu ha ha ha ha ha!

Shark, me hearties.

Shark!

The next morning, at ten past sunrise,
whilst Dad and Lizzie were still
safely snuggled in their beds,
a whirling, spinning, dust-spitting tornado
crashed down from the sky
and threw everything up into the air.

CRASH!

The house shook outside in and back again.

Suddenly, the branch of a silver tree

burst in through the curtains,

closely followed by a rabble

of tumbling creatures

and a bright blue straggler.

Out of the door they flew.

Lizzie threw back the covers

and set off in hot pursuit.

10

"Please tell me I'm dreaming," Dad whispered.
"No, they're for real, Dad," Lizzie whooped.

The birds stopped tweeting.
For a second they looked startled,
and then, in a blizzard of feathers,
they headed for the kitchen.

SLUGS

Great rescue, Superbird.

All in a day's chirp!

HELP

Thanks, Superbird! I was nearly toasted.

I smell a cat. We're doomed!

Toast! Pass it on.

Toast! More like singed feathers, ooh arr.

She looks friendly.

She looks dangerous.

Are we nearly there yet?

"Dad! There's a tree full of tweeting birds down here!" Lizzie squealed.
Dad would not be impressed: a hole in the roof, a huge hole in the floor and twigs everywhere!

Lizzie wasn't worried about the mess. She just wanted to make friends. "You poor things! Let me help," Lizzie cried, and set to work with the first aid kit.

She carefully picked up a very sad looking bird. "I can't mend your broken wings, but maybe you can zoom along on these instead," she said, gently slipping roller skates over the bird's claws. "I shall call you Rollerbird, if that's okay."

Bluebeak loved his new eye patch.

Crow needed his beak straightened.

How I sprained all of my feathers is a mystery!

It's not funny.

Splinters queue.

Feathers! Look, I've lost my best white-tip feather.

I've got wingpit splinters right here.

Splinters just go right through me.

Now I'm totally gorgeous.

Whatever next?

The birds waited patiently behind Rainbow Bird, who had pushed to the front for a feathers and claws manicure.

Buster noticed Lizzie befriending the birds.
His tummy purred and he decided
to become their very *special* friend too!

DIY

This nest is fantastic!

Let's live here forever!

CAT ATTACK!

Cat ahoy!

Yo ho, heave ho.

TIGER!

Troublemaker.

This nest is so luxurious. Please can we stay?

Only if we tame this beast.

Impossible!

Easy!

Somebody had to stop Buster, so Wizzling shook a wingful of magic stars from his coat and cast a special spell over the cereal.

It wasn't long before the birds began to hiccup. Their tummies started rumbling and soon they began to wizz about noisily, like jet-powered rockets, with very sharp beaks ...

... Buster didn't stand a chance!

He dived into the empty cereal packet and refused to come out.

Good afternoon, Mr Cat.

He's in the brig, ooh-arr.

COCO ZEBRAS

FREE

WE TAMED BUSTER

When Dad arrived, he was not impressed! "They've wolfed down my favourite cereal and left none for me," he grumbled.

When nests started springing up all over the house, Dad moaned about that, too. He stuck a list of things to do on the fridge door.

Lizzie found the list and made some very important changes.

Important Jobs

1. Shopping - Coco Zebras

Good idea, Dad - 10 boxes, please! xxx

tweet-proof earplugs
But I love their beautiful songs, Dad.

2. Do something about that tree!!!

But a tree in the kitchen is sooooo cool!!!

3. Nests to remove:

xx

that big scary one in my bedroom

But it'll guard your dreams, Dad.

the one sat on the toaster

It's a bird sauna, Dad.

the one hiding in the fridge

But it's for when the penguins visit!

Lots of love from Lizzie and her birdie friends xxx

Lizzie had never felt so happy. With the birds' help, she dragged the paddling pool in from the garden and all afternoon they played Pant-chutes and Pirates. It was a real tweet until ...

...Dad barged in and wanted his pants

and his kitchen utensils back.

"Those birds have stinky, beaky bad breath," Dad huffed.

"And they traipse their muddy claw prints all over the house!"

Lizzie listened to Dad's complaints and knew exactly what to do.

Just before bedtime, she ran the birds
a bubbly bath to make them sparkly clean.
Then Dad couldn't complain!

King Bubble

FEATHERS

POO

SHAM

"Goodness me!" he exclaimed, "I was going to have
a nice, relaxing bath and now they've taken all the hot water.
That does it; I've had enough!
If I get rid of that tree those pesky birds
will have to leave, too!"

Lizzie stormed to her bedroom with all of the birds flapping along behind her. They needed an amazing plan ... and fast.

Our tree is wedged in. The only way to move it is to chop it down.

But it's our new, luxury home.

We're doomed, I tell you.

"Dad's got it all wrong," Lizzie said, "but what can we do?"

We could fly south.

No, north is better.

"No! You must stay and save the tree!"

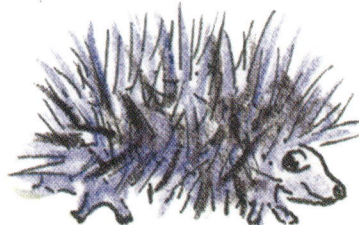

"But how can we change Dad's mind?"

Twig or tweet him!

Wizzling could use use magic to turn him into a frog.

Impossible!

Tickle-peck him!

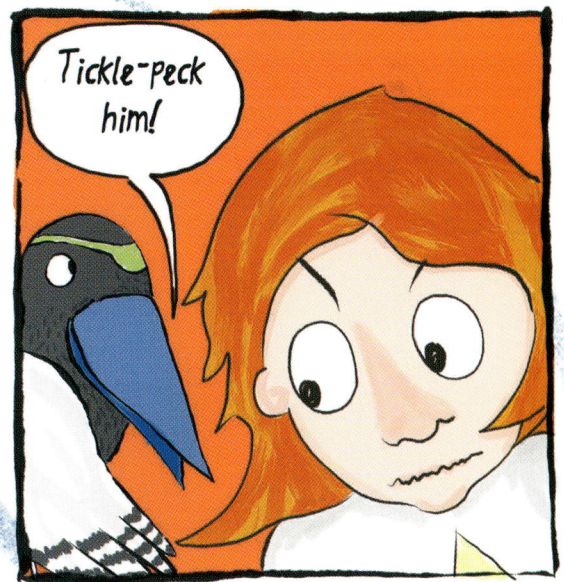

"No! We can't do that. I love my dad!"

Ghostie could haunt him until he changes his mind.

Or we could design a super-nest for us all to live in.

I will challenge him to a wrestle!

No, let's hide in the cellar!

Four minutes and forty-two seconds later:

'I've got it! Let's design a super-nest that we can all live in!' Lizzie squealed.

Great idea, Lizzie!

worms

Lizzie and the Birds' Big Plan
to Save the Tree and Transform Our Lovely House Into a Super-nest for Everyone to Share

Nest room and Coco Zebra Cafe

Worm mine

Fill cellar with soil and water the tree's roots to keep it alive.

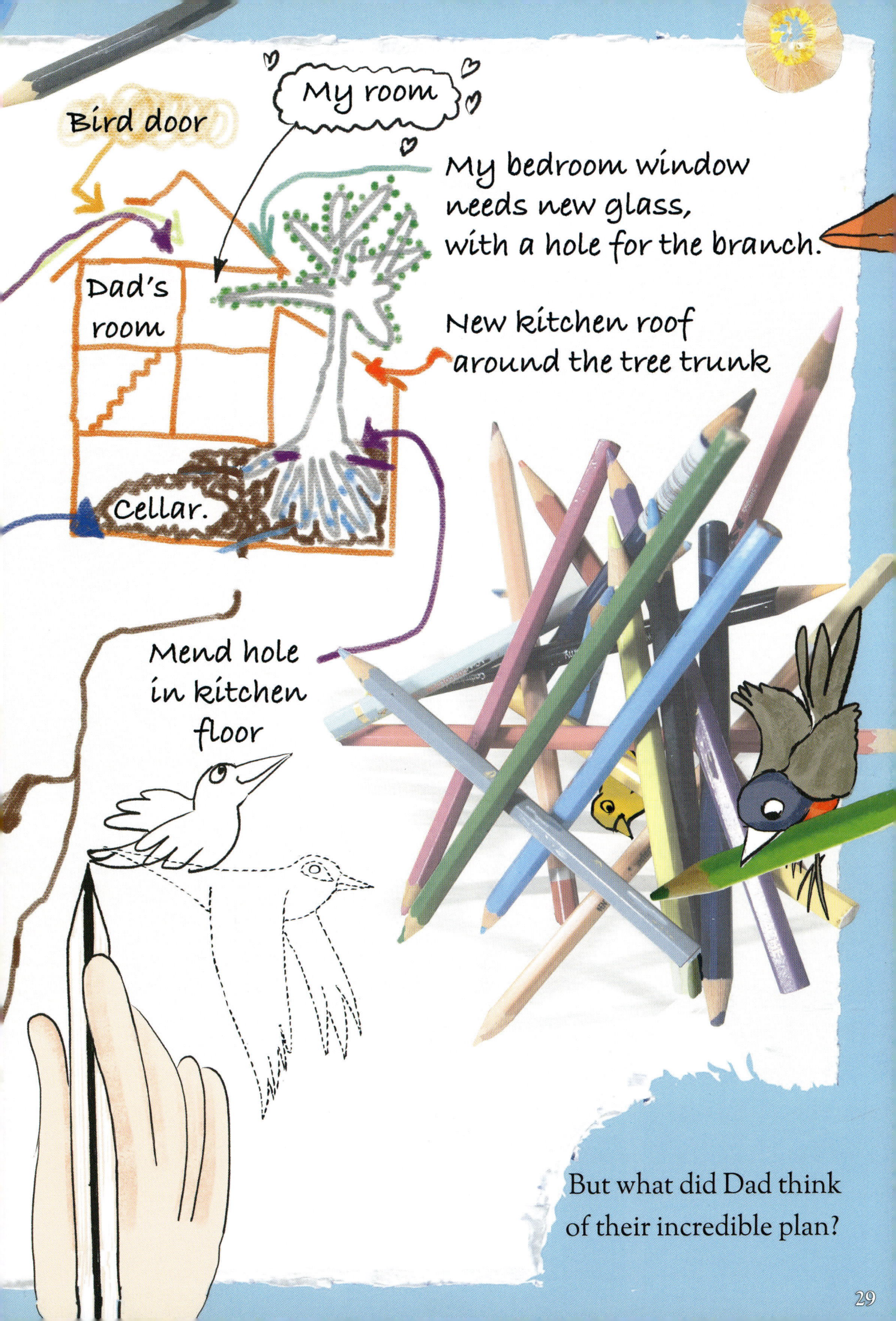

Bird door

My room

My bedroom window
needs new glass,
with a hole for the branch.

Dad's room

New kitchen roof
around the tree trunk

Cellar.

Mend hole
in kitchen
floor

But what did Dad think
of their incredible plan?

"NO! NO! NO! NO! NO!"

yelled Dad.

So Lizzie and the birds
decided to yell
even louder!
They set to work
with cardboard and paint
and then climbed up
the tree with their
messages to Dad.

COCO ZEBRAS!

THEIR HOME IS OUR HOME, DAD!

TREE IN HOUSE FOREVER!

♥ TREE

BIRDS ♥ DAD

LET'S NEST TOGETHER

BIRDS ♥ LUXURIES TOO!!!

COME AND JOIN US!

"I love my birds, Dad," Lizzie sang.
She climbed higher into the tree,
out above the kitchen roof,
but then ...

... she lost her balance.
Leaves trembled,
twigs snapped
and with a yelp
of surprise,
Lizzie fell
from the tree.

Before you could say
"abracadabra",
Wizzling cast out
a net of stars
to catch her.

What a wonderful catch it was!

Seconds later, the birds all swooped in and carried her up into the air.
"Look Dad, I'm flying!" she whooped with delight.

After two laps of the garden, the birds gently lowered Lizzie
into Dad's arms.
"Wow!" he said. "Those birds are awesome.
They saved you, Lizzie. How can I ever
thank them enough?"
"Well, we have got a really good
plan, you know" Lizzie replied
with a grin.
Dad grinned too.
It was all he needed to do.

Success!

Whoopee!

LIZZIE
ROCKS!

COOL
LIZZIE!

Birds are
the
champions!

We really are awesome!

All the feathers
in the house
say yeah!

Yeah!

Yeah!

Too heavy!

Worms.

Replanting the tree's roots
in fresh soil,
and repairing the house,
was a great team effort.

nest

Dad soon found out that
living with a tree full of birds
was a wonderful, crazy...
... adventure!

This way for more adventures!